ILLINOIS

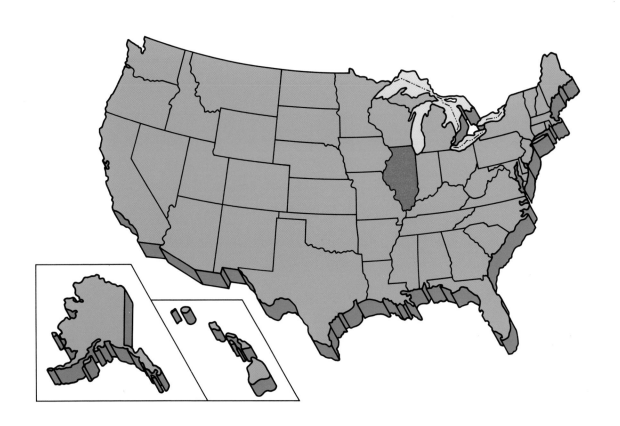

ILLINOIS

Kathy P. Anderson

 Lerner Publications Company

This book is available in two editions:
Library binding by Lerner Publications Company
Soft cover by First Avenue Editions, 1995
241 First Avenue North
Minneapolis, MN 55401
ISBN: 0–8225–2723–5 (lib. bdg.)
ISBN: 0–8225–9706–3 (pbk.)

Website address: www.lernerbooks.com

LIBRARY OF CONGRESS CATALOGING-IN-PUBLICATION DATA

Anderson, Kathy.
    Illinois / Kathy Anderson.
       p.   cm. – (Hello USA)
    Includes index.
    Summary: Introduces the state's geography,
history, environmental issues, interesting sights,
and how the people work and live.
    ISBN 0–8225–2723–5 (lib. bdg.)
    1. Illinois—Juvenile literature.
[1. Illinois.] I. Title. II. Series.
F541.3.A53   1992
977.3—dc20   91–41223

Manufactured in the United States of America
3 4 5 6 7 8 – JR – 02 01 00 99 98 97

Cover photography courtesy of
Ed Lee / Root Resources.

The glossary that begins on page
68 gives definitions of words
shown in **bold type** in the text.

CONTENTS

Did You Know . . . ?

☐ The people of Metropolis, Illinois, claim that their town is the home of the legendary Superman. Pictures of the cartoon character appear on the town's water tower and on a billboard at the town's entrance. From the city's official Superman phone booth you can even talk to Superman!

☐ Western Avenue in Chicago is the longest continuous city street in the world—it goes on for 24.5 miles (39.5 kilometers).

☐ Chicago's Sears Tower is the tallest building in the world. In fact, Chicago is home to three of the world's five tallest skyscrapers.

Squirrels live in most cities in Illinois. But the town of Olney is home to many white squirrels. In 1902 a boy named Thomas Tippitt set free a pair of the unusual animals. The male was killed, but the female soon appeared with babies.

The white squirrel population has grown into the hundreds. Olney protects the animals with special laws. White squirrels always have the right of way on streets in Olney, and no one may take a white squirrel out of town.

YOU ARE NOW LEAVING OLNEY

A Trip
Around the State

In the midwestern United States lies Illinois, the Prairie State. Cornfields and pastures stretch for miles across Illinois's long horizon. In the northeastern corner, skyscrapers taller than the tallest hills in the state break the horizon. The buildings are part of Chicago, the third largest city in the United States.

Some people think that Chicago is Illinois. This sprawling urban area dwarfs the cities and towns around it. But there is much more to the state than its largest city.

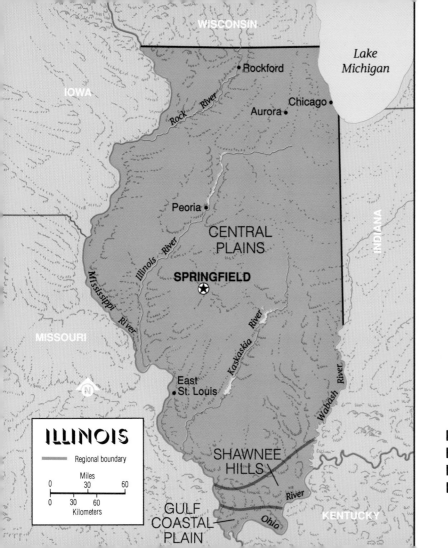

Five states border
Illinois—Wisconsin, Iowa,
Missouri, Kentucky, and
Indiana.

Water hems in much of Illinois. Lake Michigan—one of the five **Great Lakes**—laps against the state's northeastern corner. Along western Illinois, the Mississippi River carves a squiggly boundary. The Ohio River flows along southern Illinois, and the Wabash River marks part of the state's eastern edge.

The mighty Mississippi glides past the farmland of west central Illinois.

Water, in the form of **glaciers**, also shaped Illinois's largest land region—the Central Plains. Glaciers, or huge sheets of ice, crept over most of the area thousands of years ago, flattening the land in their path. When the glaciers melted, they left ground-up rock and clay, which now make up the rich soil of the Central Plains.

The flat, fertile plains of the region stretch from Illinois's northern border almost to its southern tip. At one time the region was a

Though much of Illinois is flat and covered with cornfields, steep rock formations are found in the Shawnee Hills region.

prairie (grassland), but now most of it is planted with corn and soybeans. The northwestern corner of the Central Plains, untouched by glaciers, has rolling hills and valleys. Rich deposits of coal lie in the southwestern half of the region.

The glaciers stopped before they reached the Shawnee Hills, a region just south of the Central Plains. Nature lovers enjoy the deep valleys, steep riverbanks, and forested hills of this strip of land.

13

Cypress trees soak in the waters of Horseshoe Lake in the Gulf Coastal Plain.

The very southern tip of Illinois includes part of the Gulf Coastal Plain, a large region that extends south all the way to the Gulf of Mexico (an arm of the Atlantic Ocean). Hills mark the northern section of Illinois's Gulf Coastal Plain, while the southern part is flat and swampy.

Illinois has about 500 waterways. The Illinois River, the longest inside the state, runs southwest into the Mississippi River. The Kaskaskia River in the south and the Rock River in the north also flow into the Mississippi.

Ships from all over the world unload their cargo in Chicago.

Lake Michigan touches the northeastern corner of Illinois. The lake is linked to the Saint Lawrence Seaway, which connects the Great Lakes to the Atlantic Ocean. Illinoisans send products from Lake Michigan along the seaway to the ocean and around the world. Because Chicago is connected to these important waterways, the city has become one of the nation's busiest ports.

Wild animals *(above)* **and wildflowers** *(right)* **lure Illinoisans into the woods.**

Illinois's weather changes swiftly from day to day and from season to season. Cold winds from the north and warm winds from the south often sweep over the state's flat plains, making temperatures drop or rise quickly. Summer temperatures average 75° F (24° C) in the north, but in the south temperatures average more than 80° F (27° C). In the winter, temperatures in the north usually drop below 25° F (–4° C), while they stay around 36° F (2° C) in the south.

During the spring and summer, tornadoes and thunderstorms often threaten cities and farmlands throughout Illinois. In 1917 Illinois was hit by one of the longest lasting tornadoes in history. While most tornadoes usually last less than an hour, this one lasted seven hours.

In wooded areas throughout Illinois, deer, rabbits, squirrels, raccoon, and foxes live and raise their young. Muskrat, beavers, mink, and otters build their homes and find food near the state's rivers and lakes.

Ducks and geese from the northern states and Canada pass through Illinois as they fly south for the winter and north again for the summer. The Illinois River valley is a rest area for about two million ducks.

Illinois's Story

The first people to live in what is now Illinois probably moved into the area about 12,000 years ago. These Native Americans, or American Indians, moved from place to place, hunting large animals and gathering plants for food. Around 300 B.C., another group of Native Americans came to the region. These people are now called mound builders.

The mound builders got their name from the huge earthen mounds they made. They buried their dead in some of the mounds and built temples on top of others. Important people, such as priests and chiefs, lived in the temples.

The Indians built their largest village near what is now Cahokia, Illinois. With a population of about 40,000, this village was really a city. It had a central mound, which was like the downtown area of modern cities. Surrounding this mound were five "suburbs," or clusters of wood-and-grass houses where most of the people lived. The farmers of the village grew corn, beans, and squash, while skilled craftspeople made pottery, mirrors, cups, and jewelry.

By studying skeletons of mound builders *(left)*, scientists can learn more about the people who lived at what is now Cahokia *(below)*.

Most Illinois Indians lived in the Till Plains. During the summer, fires sometimes swept the region's dry grasslands, destroying the Illinois's homes.

By A.D. 1600 the mound builders had disappeared. No one knows for certain, but they may have been wiped out by diseases or repeated crop failures.

Soon several tribes—including the Cahokia, Kaskaskia, Michigamea, Moingwena, Peoria, and Tamarou—moved into the region. These tribes were known as the Illinois, a French spelling of the Indians' word for "people." The Illinois lived in villages near river valleys. They made canoes, houses, and tools from wood. In the spring, the women planted fields of corn and beans. In the winter, the tribes left their villages to hunt buffalo.

To catch the buffalo, the Illinois sometimes surrounded a herd with a ring of fire. The hunters then shot the trapped animals with bows and arrows. The Illinois ate the buffalo meat and made the skins into clothes and blankets.

The Illinois probably first met white people in 1673, when French explorers Louis Jolliet and Jacques Marquette traveled through what is now Illinois. The explorers' trip took them down the Mississippi River and up the Illinois River to Lake Michigan.

Jolliet and Marquette were probably the first white people to explore the Mississippi and Illinois rivers.

France soon claimed the land that Jolliet and Marquette had visited, and French fur traders set up trading posts in the region. The traders gave European goods, such as iron tools and glass beads, to the Illinois in exchange for beaver pelts. Traders made lots of money by selling the pelts in Europe, where men's hats made of beaver skins were very popular.

Like the French, the British wanted the land and rich fur trade in North America for themselves. In 1754 the French and the British fought for control of North America in what became known as the French and Indian War. During the war, the Illinois and many neighboring tribes helped the French fight the British. But even with help from the Indians, the French lost the war and left the region.

The Indians were soon pushed out of the region as well. The United States claimed the Illinois area in 1784 and by the early 1800s, settlers were coming down the Ohio River from Kentucky, Virginia, and other states.

Around 1779 Jean Baptiste Pointe du Sable, a black fur trader, built a trading post near an Indian camp on the Chicago River. The first permanent settler in what became Chicago, du Sable is considered the founder of the city.

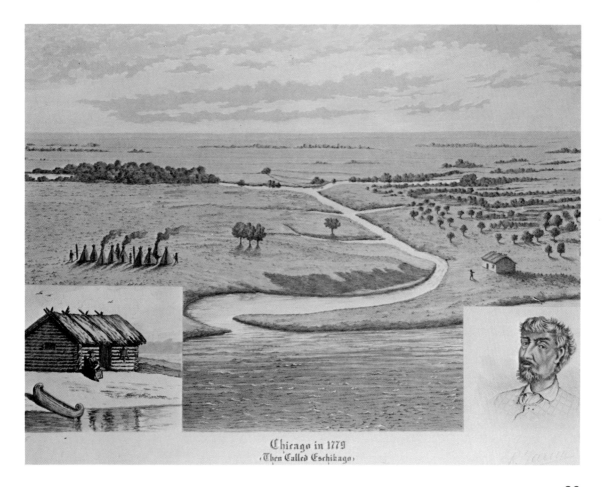

Chicago in 1779
(Then Called Eschikago)

23

The population of settlers was soon large enough for Illinois to qualify for statehood. On December 3, 1818, Illinois became the 21st state. Politicians from Illinois asked the U.S. government to move the new state's northern border 60 miles (97 km) farther north. The extended border brought a small community—Chicago—into the new state. If the border hadn't been moved, Chicago would now be in Wisconsin.

More newcomers arrived. The state's population tripled in 10 years, reaching 150,000 by 1830. Although the new settlers and U.S. troops pushed most Native Americans westward, some Indians remained in Illinois. Black Hawk, a Sauk chief and warrior, knew that his tribe had been forced to give up its land unfairly. He and his followers refused to leave their village.

The U.S. Army prepared to drive the group out of Illinois in 1832. Warriors from neighboring tribes, including the Kickapoo, Potawatomi, and Fox, joined the Sauk to fight the army in what became known as the Black Hawk War. The Native Americans were outnumbered and beaten badly in the four-month-long war. By the war's end, settlers and the U.S. government claimed all the land in Illinois.

At the Battle of Bad Axe, U.S. troops killed almost 300 of Black Hawk's followers as they tried to surrender.

In 1837 in Grand Detour, Illinois, John Deere invented a plow that cut through thick sod, allowing farmers to plant more crops.

In the 1830s and 1840s, thousands of new settlers came to Illinois. Most came from Europe and the eastern United States, where jobs and farmland were hard to find. Some of the newcomers dug canals. Others mined coal in the southern half of the state. Many built farms and planted corn in the prairie soil of central Illinois.

These farmers profited when the Illinois and Michigan Canal opened in 1848. The canal connected Lake Michigan to the Illinois and Mississippi rivers. Farmers in central and southern Illinois could send their crops and livestock cheaply

When grain from central and southern Illinois reached Chicago, it was cleaned and temporarily stored in buildings called grain elevators.

and quickly by water to Chicago. From there the crops were shipped across the Great Lakes to the large markets of the East Coast. Returning boats carried lumber, manufactured goods, and farm machinery to Chicago. The goods were then sent to Illinois's farmers.

Even as the canal opened, railroad crews were hammering train tracks into place. By the early 1850s, Illinois had thousands of miles of railroad tracks. Trains brought coal from southern Illinois to Chicago. The coal was then burned to fuel machines in the city's factories. The railroads also brought Irish, German, and other European **immigrants** to the state. Many immigrants built farms, but others moved to cities. These newcomers, who often came to the country with little money, were usually willing to work for low wages.

This cheap source of labor, as well as good transportation and a

Many Chicagoans worked in brickyards . . .

cheap source of coal nearby, helped industries in Chicago to boom. Cattle and hogs from Illinois's farms were transported to Chicago's stockyards, where the animals were fattened and then butchered. Illinois's farmers also sent their corn to Chicago, where it was weighed and stored in grain elevators. The meat and grain were shipped from Chicago by boat or train to eastern markets.

Chicago's lumberyards bought trees from Wisconsin, then cut the timber into boards and sold it to the city's furniture factories. The factories sent the finished furniture to farms and towns west of the Mississippi River.

... or in lumberyards. The boards and bricks they made were used to pave streets and build houses in Chicago and other growing cities in the United States.

The Lincoln-Douglas Debates

In 1854 Senator Stephen Douglas of Illinois introduced the Kansas-Nebraska Act. This law allowed settlers in the western United States to decide whether they wanted slavery to be legal in their territories. Many people were afraid that this act would allow slavery to spread throughout the west.

Abraham Lincoln, a lawyer from Springfield, Illinois, agreed with these people. In 1858 he ran against Douglas for a seat in the U.S. Senate. The two men argued about slavery in a series of debates, or discussions, held in seven Illinois towns. Lincoln lost the election, but he proved himself a great speaker. He became so famous for his strong arguments against slavery that he was chosen to run for U.S. president in 1860. This time he won.

While Illinois and other Northern states earned money making goods in factories, the Southern states relied on farming for their money. Many Southern farmers used slaves to work the land. Southern politicians argued that this was the only way Southern farmers could make a profit.

But in Northern states, such as Illinois, slavery was illegal. Many people wanted to outlaw slavery in every state. Southerners feared that one of those people was Abraham Lincoln, an Illinoisan who was elected U.S. president in 1860.

Soon after Lincoln's election, the Southern states decided to form a new country—the Confederate States of America—where slavery would remain legal. In 1861 President Lincoln sent Union, or Northern, troops to keep the United States together. The Civil War had begun. In Illinois, factories made weapons and farmers grew food for Union soldiers, who won the war in 1865.

Abraham Lincoln

After the Civil War, more factories were built all over Illinois, creating many new jobs. Immigrants from Poland, Italy, and other European countries moved to Chicago, where they found jobs making iron and steel, radios, candy, and soap.

When immigrants came to Chicago, they usually moved into neighborhoods with people from their native country.

The Great Chicago Fire

The summer of 1871 was the driest in Chicago's history. Wood buildings and wood sidewalks were all dry as a bone. So when Mrs. Patrick O'Leary's cow kicked over an oil lamp on October 8, 1871, the fire that started in the cow's barn spread quickly to nearby homes and soon flamed out of control. The fire burned so brightly that the sky was as light as day. A blizzard of burning sparks flew from the fire, lighting small fires wherever they landed and blistering animals and people. The air around the fire was so hot that houses burst into flames before the fire even reached them. The Great Chicago Fire destroyed 2,000 acres (810 hectares) of the city, left more than 100,000 people homeless, and reduced $200 million worth of property to ashes. Only two public buildings—the water tower and the pumping station—survived the fire.

Coal from southern Illinois was sent by rail *(above)* to industries such as the lace factories *(left)* in Zion and the stockyards *(top)* of East Saint Louis and Chicago.

The eagle on Illinois's flag sits on a boulder in a prairie. Flying from the eagle's beak is a banner imprinted with the state motto. The date 1818 refers to the year Illinois became a state, and 1868 is the year the state seal was chosen.

East Saint Louis, Illinois, became the site of giant steel-making and oil-cleaning factories. In Joliet, Moline, and Rock Island, workers built farm machines that helped farmers raise more crops.

When World War I started in Europe in 1914, factories in Illinois operated at full speed to make weapons and tanks. There was so much to do that more workers were needed.

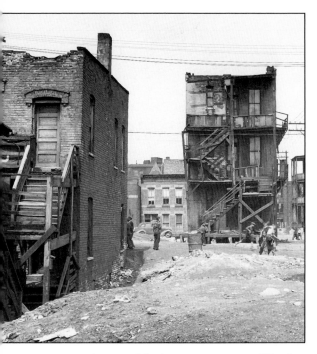

Although most black newcomers to Illinois moved to Chicago *(above),* there were black communities in many cities. Tension between white and black people grew, and in the early 1900s riots broke out in Springfield, East Saint Louis, and Chicago.

Black people living in southern states heard of the jobs in Chicago and began moving north. Chicago's black population soon tripled. Because whites would not sell homes or rent apartments in much of the city to blacks, most black people squeezed into a few small, rundown neighborhoods. After the war ended in 1918, African Americans continued to arrive in Chicago, looking for jobs. But they were usually offered the lowest paying jobs in the city.

Prohibition, a set of laws that made the producing and selling of liquor a crime, was passed in 1920. Gangsters in Chicago became rich and powerful by supplying liquor to the city's 20,000 illegal bars, called **speakeasies**. Gangsters also operated illegal gambling parlors. Al Capone was one of the most famous of Chicago's gangsters. Capone was arrested in 1936, just three years after Prohibition ended. But many gangsters remained powerful for years to come.

Gangsters often fought each other for control of liquor sales. In the era's most famous murders, known as the Saint Valentine's Day massacre, gangsters disguised as police killed seven members of a rival gang.

In January 1937 the Ohio River overflowed its banks and flooded the southern tip of Illinois. Eight counties were underwater during what became known as the Great Flood of 1937. In Shawneetown *(above)* few homes survived the flood.

In 1941 U.S. troops went to war in Europe. During World War II, Illinois's factories were busier than ever before. In Chicago, Rockford, Moline, Peoria, Springfield, and East Saint Louis, workers made planes, bombs, tanks, and other goods needed for the war. Farmers sent tons of grain overseas to feed the soldiers.

During World War II, a factory in Illinois made earth movers to send to soldiers in Europe.

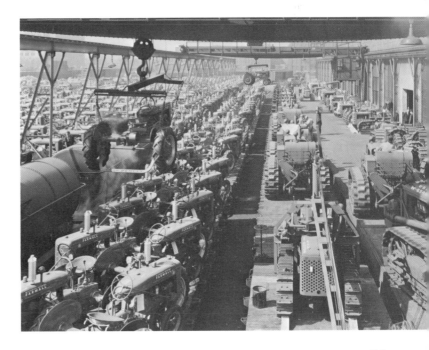

10,000 B.C. | **A.D.1673** | **1779** | **1818** | **1832** | **1848** | **1858** | **1871**

People first enter what is now Illinois

Jolliet and Marquette travel up the Illinois River

du Sable builds the settlement that becomes Chicago

Illinois becomes the 21st state

Black Hawk War

Illinois and Michigan Canal opens

Lincoln-Douglas debates

Great Chicago Fire

After the war, manufacturing continued to grow, but the number of farms dropped by half, as farmers left their fields for higher paying jobs in factories. By the 1970s, however, many factories and other businesses began leaving Illinois for states where companies could be run more cheaply.

Chicago's population dropped as people with enough money moved to the suburbs, leaving behind the city's crime, run-down neighborhoods, and overcrowded schools. Illinoisans are now struggling to balance the needs of all the people in their state, from the inner city to the farm.

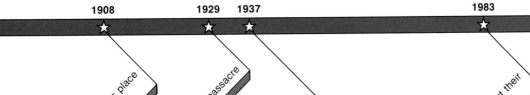

1908 — Rioting takes place in Springfield

1929 — Saint Valentine's Day massacre

1937 — Great Flood

1983 — Chicagoans elect their first black mayor

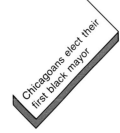

Harold Washington became the first African American mayor of Chicago in 1983 and served until his death in 1987.

41

Living and Working in Illinois

Of the 11.5 million people in Illinois, more than half live in or around Chicago. Rows of skyscrapers, including three of the world's five tallest buildings, line the city's downtown. Beyond Chicago, though, Illinois takes on a different look. Tractors replace commuter trains, and skyscrapers become stalks of corn. There are other cities in Illinois, too. Of these, Rockford, Peoria, Springfield, and Aurora are the biggest.

Many Illinoisans choose to live in Chicago *(facing page)* **or one of its suburbs, while others stay in small towns such as Cobden** *(above)* **in southwestern Illinois.**

In Illinois, about 15 percent of the people are African American, 8 percent are Hispanic and 3 percent are Asian. Almost everyone else in the state has ancestors from Ireland, Poland, Russia, Germany, Italy, Sweden, and other European countries.

Two young Illinoisans enjoy painting outdoors.

When Illinois became a state, almost all Illinoisans were farmers. Though three-fourths of Illinois's land is still used for crops, less than 2 percent of Illinoisans work on farms, and farmers earn only 2 percent of the state's money.

More corn and soybeans are grown in the state than any other crop. Illinois is one of the top soybean producers in the nation. Other crops include wheat, oats, and sorghum (a cereal grain). Farmers in northern Illinois plant asparagus, beans, and cabbage. Many farmers also raise hogs, sheep, and cattle.

Although mining earns less than 1 percent of the state's money, Illinois produces more coal than all but four other states. In the southern half of Illinois, 60 million tons (54 million metric tons) of coal are dug up every year.

Illinois earns 19 percent of its money from manufacturing. Many Illinoisans build machines that are used all over the world. Moline and Peoria have some of the world's biggest manufacturers of farm and construction equipment. Factories in Normal and Belvidere produce cars, and factories in Freeport and Mount Vernon make tires.

Other manufacturers in the state process crops and livestock into food products such as breakfast cereal, sausage, and candy. In the

Workers assemble a huge tractor at a factory in Moline.

Chicago area, people package medicines and cleaning solutions. Illinoisans also print books and newspapers. The largest printing company in the United States is in Chicago.

Illinois sells many of its products throughout the world. More goods are bought and sold at the Chicago Board of Trade than anywhere else in the world. Buyers and sellers in Chicago trade millions of tons of grain, cattle, eggs, coal, oil, and other products each year. Truck drivers, train engineers, ship captains, and airplane pilots move tons of crops, coal, and manufactured goods from Illinois to markets outside the state.

A tugboat pushes a barge down the Illinois River.

People who trade or transport goods are called service workers because they provide a service to other people or businesses. Three-fourths of all working Illinoisans have some kind of service job, including mayors, teachers, nurses, salespeople, and bankers. Some service workers sell tickets and move luggage at Chicago-O'Hare International Airport, the world's busiest airfield. Every day, about 1,500 planes land on or take off from its runways.

Fire fighters are service workers who sometimes risk their lives to help save others.

When Illinoisans aren't working, many of them like to go swimming, fishing, or boating on the state's lakes and rivers. Chicagoans play on the beaches along Lake Michigan and bicycle and picnic in the city's parks. Many Illinoisans hike over the hills and through the valleys of the Shawnee National Forest in southern Illinois.

Athletes *(top left)* **sprint to start a swimming race. A Chicago Cub** *(above)* **waits for the ball.**

49

The Time Museum in Rockford holds timepieces like this one, which is over 2,500 years old.

Baseball fans cheer for one of Illinois's two major league teams—the Chicago White Sox, who play at Comiskey Park, and the Chicago Cubs, who play at Wrigley Field. Football fans follow the Chicago Bears at Soldier Field. The Black Hawks, the professional hockey team, and the Bulls, of the National Basketball Association, both play in the Chicago Stadium.

Illinois boasts many museums and historic sites. Chicago is home to the Art Institute of Chicago, the Adler Planetarium, and the John G. Shedd Aquarium. Visitors to Chicago can explore a life-size copy of a coal mine at the Museum of Science and Industry and dinosaur skeletons at the Field Museum of Natural History. The DuSable Museum of African American History, one of the finest of its kind in the country, is also in Chicago. In Rockford, the Time Museum displays thousands of clocks, some of which are 3,000 years old.

Visitors to the Kohl Children's Museum in Wilmette can learn about science by making soap bubbles *(above)*. At the Adler Planetarium *(top right)* in Chicago, people see stars, even in the daytime. Animals from all over the world live at Brookfield Zoo *(right)*.

Galena, a city in northwestern Illinois, has been restored to look as it did in the 1800s, when it was a booming mining town. The Cahokia Mounds near Collinsville and the Black Hawk statue near Oregon remind visitors of Illinois's earliest residents. Monuments to Abraham Lincoln attract tourists to New Salem and to Springfield in central Illinois. Springfield, the state's capital, also hosts the Illinois State Fair every year.

Chicago offers a variety of festivals and parades, including the Polish Day parade, the Chicago Jazz Festival, the Saint Patrick's Day Parade, Scandinavian Week, the International Folk Fair, and DanceAfrica, a week-long celebration of African music and dance. Illinoisans can sample the food at the Chili Shootout in East Moline. Native American dances, food, and stories are featured at Black Hawk Days in Rock Island.

Garbage is often hidden from view. In fact, people throw away more garbage than you can probably imagine. Each person in Illinois, for instance, creates an average of more than a ton of waste every year.

Protecting the Environment

Illinois has a lot of people for a state its size. Twenty-five states are larger than Illinois, but only five have higher populations. Illinois's many people and the companies they work for need water and land to survive. But the waste people and industries create threatens these limited natural resources.

The factories, businesses, and people in Illinois produce millions of tons of waste every year. In fact, each Illinoisan throws away an average of 6.2 pounds (2.8 kilograms) of **solid waste** each day. Magazines, food, grass cuttings, furniture, used appliances, and packaging material are all solid waste.

Some of this trash can be recycled. In fact, many scientists think that we could recycle more than 50 percent of all solid waste. But in 1995 only about 21 percent of Illinois's solid waste was recycled. Thirteen million tons of trash went into **landfills.**

Empty landfills are shaped like enormous bathtubs. Waste is dumped into the landfill, packed down, and covered with dirt or a special kind of foam. When rain falls on a landfill, the rain mixes with rotting garbage to form a liquid called **leachate.**

At the bottom of most landfills is a liner, usually a huge sheet of plastic with clay underneath it, which keeps the leachate from seeping into the ground. But the liner can crack or split, allowing leachate to leak. The leachate then carries pollutants through the soil under the landfill to **groundwater** and to nearby rivers and lakes. When people or wildlife drink the poisoned water, they can get sick or die.

Even if landfills were completely safe, Illinoisans would still have a garbage problem. Sixty-two landfills in the state have room for more trash. If no new landfills are built, the state's existing landfills will be overflowing by the year 2005. Illinoisans need to find other ways to get rid of their solid waste.

A bulldozer in a landfill crushes waste so the garbage will take up less room.

One way to control waste is to reduce the amount of trash produced. For example, people can ask to stop getting magazines, mail-order catalogs, or telephone directories that they don't need. When shopping, people can choose items without lots of cardboard or plastic packaging, so less material will be thrown away.

Another way to cut down on waste is to buy goods that can be reused. Rather than buying plastic or paper cups and containers, which are thrown away after one use, people can use glass and ceramic cups and plates. A group of families or friends can buy one copy of a magazine or newspaper to share.

Recycling trash also reduces solid waste. People can choose to buy

When glass is recycled, it is broken into pieces, melted down, and shaped into new glass.

items packaged in recyclable materials. This encourages manufacturers to package their products in recyclable materials. Glass, aluminum foil, tin cans, paper, and plastic can all be recycled. Food scraps, grass clippings, and leaves can be recycled in a compost pile— a mixture of rotting vegetation that is saved to fertilize soil.

Illinois is working to make less solid waste. In 1990 the state government banned yard waste from landfills. Instead of throwing grass clippings and leaves in the trash, residents must leave them on the lawn or put them in a compost pile. And by law, every county in Illinois must recycle 25 percent of its waste by the late 1990s.

Some towns put their leaves on a compost pile, which will later be used as fertilizer.

A student in Freeburg, Illinois, helps her school's recycling program.

Cities throughout Illinois have already begun to pick up recyclables—newspapers, cans, and plastic—from homes and businesses. Schools in Illinois are required by law to teach students how to reduce and recycle.

Illinois has a long way to go before it solves its solid-waste problem. The state will eventually run out of room in its landfills. But if everyone works to reduce and recycle now, Illinois will be able to handle its waste further into the future.

By cutting down on their trash, Illinoisans hope to preserve nature.

Illinois's Famous People

HARRISON FORD

ACTORS

Harrison Ford (born 1942) played Han Solo in the three *Star Wars* movies. Some of his other films include *Raiders of the Lost Ark* and *Indiana Jones and the Temple of Doom*. Ford is from Chicago.

Richard Pryor (born 1940), from Peoria, has acted in many films, including *Stir Crazy*. But Pryor is probably best known as a stand-up comic and has won five Grammy Awards for his comedy albums.

Robin Williams (born 1952), from Chicago, has acted in many movies, including *Dead Poets Society, Awakenings,* and *Hook*. He also played Mork on the television show "Mork and Mindy."

◀ MARSHALL FIELD

RICHARD PRYOR ▶

▲ ROBIN WILLIAMS

BUSINESS LEADERS

Philip Armour (1832–1901) started Armour and Company, a huge meat-packing operation, in Chicago. He was known for making his meat products out of "every part of the pig but the squeal."

Marshall Field (1834–1906) moved to Chicago when he was 22. There, he founded Marshall Field & Company, a department store. He was the first store owner in the country to allow unhappy customers to exchange their purchases.

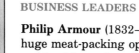

PHILIP ARMOUR ▶

62

Ray Kroc (1902–1984) bought a small fast-food restaurant called McDonald's from two Californians in the 1950s. Kroc reopened McDonald's in Des Plaines, Illinois, and turned it into a chain of restaurants, which have now expanded throughout the world.

GANGSTER

Al Capone (1899–1947) moved from New York to Chicago in 1919. He was soon in charge of a gang of criminals. He controlled the gambling and the supply of liquor in the city, and his gang often got into bloody gunfights with other gangs. In 1931 he went to prison for cheating on his taxes.

▲ AL CAPONE

▲ ENRICO FERMI

INVENTORS

Enrico Fermi (1901–1954) came to the United States from Italy in 1938, the year he won a Nobel Prize in physics. At the University of Chicago he and his team of scientists learned how to release nuclear energy, which made the development of the nuclear bomb possible.

George Ferris (1859–1896) of Galesburg, Illinois, built the world's largest "pleasure wheel" in 1893. It was 250 feet (76 meters) high. The pleasure wheels soon became known as Ferris wheels in honor of Ferris.

MUSICIANS

Miles Davis (1926–1990) was born in Alton, Illinois. A trumpet player, he recorded famous albums such as *Kind of Blue* and *Miles Ahead*. Davis played a major role in creating new styles of jazz after the 1940s.

Benny Goodman (1909–1986), a jazz clarinet player and a bandleader, is known as the King of Swing. Goodman, who was a Chicagoan, won a Grammy Award for his life achievement in music in 1985.

Mahalia Jackson (1911–1972) moved to Chicago at the age of 15 and started her career as a gospel singer one year later. Her albums and concerts made gospel music popular throughout the country. She also worked to gain equal rights for African Americans.

◄ MILES DAVIS

▲ BENNY GOODMAN

◄ MAHALIA JACKSON

◄ RICHARD DALEY

STEPHEN ▼ DOUGLAS

POLITICAL LEADERS

Richard Daley (1902–1976) was the mayor of Chicago from 1955 to his death. He was famous for his complete control of Chicago's government. He rewarded his supporters with jobs and kept his enemies from gaining power.

Stephen A. Douglas (1813–1861) represented Illinois in the U.S. House of Representatives and the U.S. Senate for 17 years. He ran for U.S. president in 1860 but was defeated by Abraham Lincoln.

Abraham Lincoln (1809–1865) started his career as a politician in New Salem, Illinois, and later practiced law in Springfield.

He became the U.S. president in 1861 and freed the slaves in the Southern states during the Civil War one year later.

SOCIAL LEADERS

Jane Addams (1860–1935), born in Cedarville, Illinois, founded Hull House with a friend in 1889. The house provided child care, classes for children and adults, and other services for the immigrant families who lived in Chicago's slums. Addams also created the first playground in Chicago.

Ida B. Wells (1862–1931) moved to Chicago in 1893. She wrote editorials and made speeches about the rights of both women and African Americans. She started the country's first group for black women seeking the right to vote.

▲ ABRAHAM LINCOLN

◀ JANE ADDAMS

GWENDOLYN
▼ BROOKS

WRITERS

Gwendolyn Brooks (1917) grew up in Chicago. In 1950 she won a Pulitzer Prize for *Annie Allen*, a book of poems. Brooks, the poet laureate (outstanding poet) of Illinois, was the first African American to win the Pulitzer.

Edgar Rice Burroughs (1875–1950), born in Chicago, introduced his character Tarzan in 1912. He went on to write 26 books about Tarzan. Tarzan stories have been made into movies and programs for radio and television.

Shel Silverstein (born 1932) is an author, cartoonist, and composer from Chicago. His writings and drawings are featured in his popular books—*Where the Sidewalk Ends, A Light in the Attic,* and *The Giving Tree.*

Facts-at-a-Glance

Nickname: Land of Lincoln
Song: "Illinois"
Motto: State Sovereignty, National Union
Flower: native violet
Tree: white oak
Bird: cardinal

Population: 11,430,602*
Rank in population, nationwide: 6th
Area: 57,918 sq mi (150,000 sq km)
Rank in area, nationwide: 25th
Date & ranking of statehood:
   December 3, 1818, the 21st state
Capital: Springfield
Major cities (and populations*):
   Chicago (2,783,726), Rockford (139,426),
   Peoria (113,504), Springfield (105,227),
   Aurora (99,581)
U.S. senators: 2
U.S. representatives: 22
Electoral votes: 24

Places to visit: Cahokia Mounds State Historic Site near Collinsville, McDonald's Museum in Des Plaines, Ulysses S. Grant Home State Historic Site in Galena, Lincoln Home National Historic Site in Springfield, Museum of Science and Industry in Chicago

Annual events: Saint Patrick's Day Parade in Chicago (March), Taste of Chicago (June), Steamboat Days and Race in Peoria (June), Pumpkin Festival in Sycamore (Oct.), International Folk Fair in Chicago (Nov.)

*1990 census

66

Natural resources: soil, coal, oil, clay, limestone, fluorspar, sand, gravel

Agricultural products: corn, soybeans, hay, wheat, barley, sorghum, hogs, beef cattle, flowers, apples

Manufactured goods: construction equipment, farm machinery, food products, electrical equipment, medicines, chemicals, cars, books and newspapers

ENDANGERED SPECIES

Mammals—Rafinesque's big-eared bat, river otter, white-tailed jackrabbit

Birds—pied-billed grebe, little blue heron, sharp-shinned hawk, greater prairie chicken

Reptiles and Amphibians—Illinois mud turtle, river cooter, dusky salamander

Fish—bigeye chub, pugnose shiner, greater redhorse, northern madtom

Plants—water pennywort, woolly milkweed, wild lettuce, cuckooflower, squirting cucumber

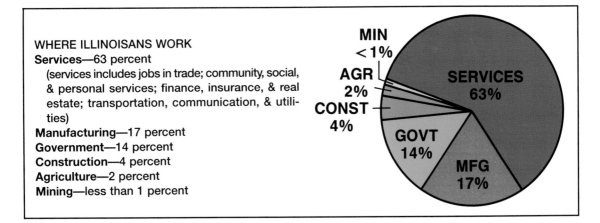

WHERE ILLINOISANS WORK
Services—63 percent
(services includes jobs in trade; community, social, & personal services; finance, insurance, & real estate; transportation, communication, & utilities)
Manufacturing—17 percent
Government—14 percent
Construction—4 percent
Agriculture—2 percent
Mining—less than 1 percent

MIN
< 1%
AGR
2%
CONST
4%
SERVICES
63%
GOVT
14%
MFG
17%

Glossary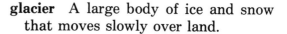

glacier A large body of ice and snow that moves slowly over land.

Great Lakes A chain of five lakes in Canada and the northern United States. They are Lakes Superior, Michigan, Huron, Erie, and Ontario.

groundwater Water that lies beneath the earth's surface. The water comes from rain and snow that seep through soil into the cracks and other openings in rocks. Groundwater supplies wells and springs.

immigrant A person who moves into a foreign country and settles there.

landfill A place specially prepared for burying solid waste.

leachate Liquid that has seeped through waste or that forms when waste rots in a landfill. Leachate can contaminate water or soil.

prairie A large area of level or gently rolling grassy land with few trees.

solid waste Useless or unwanted solid and semisolid materials that have been thrown away. Solid waste includes dry waste, food waste, yard waste, ashes, industrial waste, appliances, furniture, and construction waste.

speakeasy A place where alcoholic beverages are sold illegally.

Index

Acknowledgments:

Maryland Cartographics, Inc., pp. 2, 10; Robert Tyszka © 1992, pp. 2–3, 60; Metropolis Planet Photo, p. 6; Jack Lindstrom, p. 7; David Atherly Johnson, pp. 8, 49 (left); Illinois Department of Commerce and Community Affairs, pp. 9, 13 (inset), 43, 48, 51 (top right, bottom right); Kent & Donna Dannen, p. 11; Scott Berner/Visuals Unlimited, pp. 12–13; Gail Nachel/Root Resources, p. 14; Martin J. Schmidt/Root Resources, p. 15; Alan G. Nelson/Root Resources, p. 16 (left); Phyllis Cerny, pp. 16 (right), 44; Loren M. Root/Root Resources, p. 19 (left); Cahokia Mounds State Historic Site, p. 19 (right); Illinois State Historical Library, pp. 20, 27, 62 (bottom left), p. 63 (top), 64 (top right, bottom left); Missouri Historical Society, J. N. Marchland (neg. Events 4a), p. 21; Chicago Historical Society, pp. 23, 32, 37; Independent Picture Service, p. 25, 65 (bottom right); Deere & Company, pp. 26, 46; Lake County (IL) Museum, Regional History Archives, pp. 28, 34 (left); Library of Congress, pp. 29, 30, 31, 33, 36, 38, 39, 64 (bottom right); Lake County (IL) Museum, Curt Teich Postcard Archives, p. 34 (top right, bottom right); UPI/Bettmann Newsphotos, p. 41; Bruce S. Cushing/Visuals Unlimited, p. 42; Terry Farmer, pp. 45, 70; Irene Z. Meyers/Root Resources, p. 47; Stephen Green, p. 49 (right); The Time Museum, Rockford, Illinois, p. 50; Kevin Horan, Kohl Children's Museum, Wilmette, IL, p. 51 (top left); City of Chicago, Mayor Richard M. Daley, pp. 53, 69; Tom Hecht/Illinois Department of Energy and Natural Resources (ENR), Springfield, Illinois, p. 54; Jerry Boucher, pp. 57, 58, 59; Southern Illinois Tourism Council, p. 61; Hollywood Book and Poster, Inc., p. 62 (top, center right, center left); Armour and Company, p. 62 (bottom right); University of Chicago, p. 63 (bottom); CBS Records, p. 64 (top left); Station KSTP—Minneapolis, p. 64 (center); Minneapolis Public Library and Information Center, p. 65 (top, bottom left); Jean Matheny, p. 66.